C000039177

LEWISHAM
AND
DEPTFORD
IN OLD PHOTOGRAPHS

John Coulter

LADYWELL FIELDS.

LEWISHAM
AND
DEPTFORD
IN OLD PHOTOGRAPHS

COLLECTED BY
JOHN COULTER

ALAN SUTTON

Alan Sutton Publishing Limited
Phoenix Mill · Far Thrupp · Stroud · Gloucestershire

First Published 1990
Reprinted with corrections 1992

Copyright © John Coulter 1990

All rights reserved. No part of this publication may be reproduced, stored in a
retrieval system, or transmitted, in any form or by any means, electronic,
mechanical, photocopying, recording or otherwise, without the prior
permission of the publishers and copyright holders.

British Library Cataloguing in Publication Data

Coulter, John *1951–*
Lewisham and Deptford in old photographs.
1. London. Lewisham (London Borough), history
I. Title
942.163

ISBN 0-86299-856-5

Typeset in 9/10 Korinna.
Typesetting and origination by
Alan Sutton Publishing Limited.
Printed in Great Britain by
The Bath Press, Avon

CONTENTS

A Christmas Present For My Parents.

INTRODUCTION

Lewisham and Deptford have been yoked together since 1965 by the whim of a royal commission. The Local Government Act of 1963, passed by a Conservative government, and brought into effect by a Labour one, killed off the two metropolitan boroughs (which had been established in 1900) and created the present London Borough of Lewisham. Yet the areas had little in common, and their histories were very different.

The old fishing village of Deptford, or West Greenwich, which had engaged in some ship repairing, at least, in the fifteenth century, became an important shipbuilding centre when Henry VIII founded a royal dockyard and naval storehouse there in 1513. This attracted private shipbuilding and other heavy industry, and Deptford soon grew into a town. John Evelyn wrote of it at the beginning of the eighteenth century that 'by the increase of Buildings may be seene, that the Towne is in 80 years become neere as big as Bristoll'. Deptford was prosperous in times of war and expansion, but correspondingly poor when peace and retrenchment followed.

The most solid memorial to Deptford's wealthy and confident periods is St Paul's church, one of the baroque masterpieces of London. It completely overshadows the old parish church of St Nicholas. The recently more frequent periods of unemployment and poverty have left all too many traces. When St Paul's church was completed in 1730 a separate parish was created for it, which included an exact half of the rateable value of Deptford, but more than nine-tenths of its area, much of it farmland or marsh. With the growth of the district over the following century and a half, St Paul's became immensely more wealthy and populous than the old riverside parish of St Nicholas. At the creation of the metropolitan boroughs in 1900 St Paul's became the Borough of Deptford, but, to keep the populations more nearly equal, St Nicholas was made part of Greenwich. I have ignored the artificial division in this book, as I have the equally eccentric partition of Blackheath between Lewisham and Greenwich.

Most of what I have said about Deptford is applicable only to the older parts of the town, north of New Cross Road. Brockley and Hatcham, in the south of St Paul's parish, remained largely agricultural until the middle of the nineteenth century, when they began to be developed as areas of good quality middle-class housing. Socially, they had more in common with Lewisham than with the rest of Deptford, and economically their links were with the City of London, where many Hatcham and Brockley residents worked. It was this that led the Prince of Wales, later Edward VII, to condemn the indifference of Deptford's wealthy suburbs to the poverty of the old town.

Lewisham's history has been quite unlike Deptford's. It consisted of the two old parishes of St Mary, Lewisham, and St Margaret, Lee, which were combined as the Metropolitan Borough of Lewisham in 1900. There was no difficulty about this, as the two communities were very much alike. Lewisham had a little light industry in the eighteenth century, based on the water mills along the River Ravensbourne. They were mostly corn mills, but were also used at different times to make such diverse products as cutlery, leather, glass and rifles. But basically Lewisham and Lee were collections of farming villages and hamlets, only distinguished from the average by their proximity to London. This had two major effects. In the first place it influenced the type of agriculture, which, because there was such a ready sale for luxury fruits and vegetables in London, had a strong bias towards market gardening. More importantly, it made Lewisham and Lee, together with many other villages on a similar radius, very attractive as rural retreats for wealthy Londoners. The trend was started by courtiers in the sixteenth century, when the royal palace at Greenwich was in regular use. Thereafter, the wealthy settlers were predominantly London business and professional men. They bought many of the old farm houses in the villages, and when the supply ran short began to build villas on any field that became available. It was this fashion which promoted Lewisham's growth from a village into a town early in the nineteenth century.

This is a form of popularity, though, which inevitably breeds its own destruction. As new forms of transport made it ever easier to live in the suburbs and still work in the City, the population of Lewisham and Lee rose dramatically, and the rural charms that had made them desirable soon faded. By 1900 most of the area had been covered with houses. Only on the southern fringe did agriculture survive, and there it succumbed to a new wave of expansion in the 1920s. The influx of the middle and lower classes was of course the signal for the rich to move further into the country.

I have tried to illustrate all these aspects of the borough's history in this selection of photographs, though naturally the earlier stages tend to be represented in their decay. You will find pictures of the winding-up of Lewisham's agriculture, the late survivals of Deptford's industry, fine houses in their dotage. The dominant words in these sections are 'demolished', 'replaced by', 'destroyed'. The destroyers appear at their best: trains and trams in their first vigour, Board schools and picture palaces fresh from the trowel.

Lewisham was fortunate enough to have in Henry Wood an early amateur photographer of great ability. His pictures, taken between 1856 and 1860, show us the centre of the borough just before its village atmosphere was completely destroyed. At the end of the nineteenth century Deptford was equally well served by the press photographer Thankfull Sturdee. His pictures vividly record the transformation of his native town as the seventeenth- and eighteenth-century quarters were cleared to accommodate new roads, new theatres, new public buildings. The most important contributor to the book, though, was the postcard publisher William Perkins of Lee. He and his associates took thousands of photographs of the area between 1870 and 1914, and some fifty of their best efforts adorn these pages. Without the likes of Perkins, and the many anonymous photographers of the golden age of the postcard, such books as this could scarcely exist. I send my thanks to whatever dark-room they now inhabit.

It seemed best to divide the photographs into subject groups, but this classification is inevitably rough. Your house may feature in the 'Homes of the Rich and Poor' section, but it could equally well appear in a street scene, behind a royal procession, or indeed anywhere in the book. I have provided a good many cross-references, but it was impossible to note every case where comparison of two photographs would enhance the interest of each. The best advice on how to use the book must therefore be to browse at random. The order within sections usually has some pattern behind it. The street scenes, for example, are arranged geographically from north to south, the houses from richest to poorest, the wartime photographs chronologically.

A volume of this size can only offer a small selection of the historic photographs of Lewisham, and there is only room in the captions for the most basic information. I would advise those wishing to discover more about the pictures in this book, or disappointed at not finding a view of their street or house, to visit the Lewisham Local History Centre. There they will find thousands of other photographs, many of them quite equal in interest to those presented here. The centre's address is The Manor House, Old Road, Lee, London, SE13. Telephone: 081–852–5050 or 081–852–7087.

The Retreat of the Rural

LADYWELL FIELDS.

LEWISHAM'S EARLIEST-KNOWN PHOTOGRAPHER was Henry Wood, the son of a wealthy woollen merchant, who took many views of the village between 1856 and 1860. He shot this idyllic scene in the garden of the workhouse. The workhouse became Lewisham hospital, under extensions to which this sylvan spot disappeared long ago.

WOOD ALSO TOOK THIS PHOTOGRAPH of the farmyard of Slagrave Farm – the meadowland on the banks of the Ravensbourne, south of Ladywell – which was leased by his father. These haystacks were near Ladywell station, in what is now Ladywell Fields.

HATCHAM MANOR FARM IN QUEEN'S ROAD, photographed c. 1880, a few years before it was demolished. The rear part of New Cross fire station now occupies the site. The view is from the garden, which is now the fire station yard.

THIS IS THE ONLY KNOWN PHOTOGRAPH OF BROCKLEY GREEN FARM, otherwise called Forest Place, which was demolished c. 1870, when the Earl of St Germains made the fields available for building. The site of the farmhouse is the small open space in front of No. 1 Stondon Park. Brockley Green, enclosed in 1810, was the land on both sides of Brockley Road between Stondon Park and The Brockley Jack. St Hilda's church, for example, stands on what was once the village green.

PRIORY FARM, which was demolished in 1877, appeared to have been built c. 1700, but the remains of a moat strongly suggested that it was the successor to a medieval house. The site is now occupied by Nos 125 to 129 Rushey Green.

THE VIEW FROM BROMLEY ROAD, CATFORD, into the yard of Sangley Farm (now the Priory House school) during the period when the Tapley family were the tenants, c. 1850 to 1895.

LEE MANOR FARM C. 1885, probably showing Mary Cordwell, the wife of Mark Cordwell the farmer, and three of their daughters. The site of the farmhouse, which was demolished c. 1907, is now taken by the gardens of Nos 34 to 36 Manor Lane Terrace.

THE YARD OF COLLEGE FARM C. 1890, when the Bowditch family were the tenants. The farmhouse was demolished c. 1925, and its site is now covered by Nos 186 and 188 Burnt Ash Hill.

THE SEVENTEENTH-CENTURY WEATHER-BOARDED AND TIMBER-FRAMED FARMHOUSE of Bellingham Farm was approached from Bromley Road by this bridge over the Ravensbourne. The site of the bridge is now between two blocks of flats, Whitchurch House and Dedham House. The site of the farmhouse is in the middle of Waterbank Road, between Nos 2 and 5. The farm lost most of its land to the Bellingham Estate in the 1920s, and the house was demolished in 1932.

SHROFFOLD'S FARM C. 1916, when tenanted by Henry Panter and Sons. It was pulled down in 1927, and the site is now occupied by No. 229 Reigate Road, Downham.

WHITEFOOT LANE, seen here c. 1900, originated as an access road for Shroffold's Farm, and remained a delightful rural backwater until the 1930s. Even after the present severely modern highway was built, a fragment of the old twisting lane was left behind like an ox-bow lake, and can still be enjoyed in Forster Park.

THE YARD OF BURNT ASH FARM in the 1890s, when William Hurman Carter was the farmer. United Dairies took over the premises, at the junction of St Mildred's Road and Baring Road, in the 1920s. Some of the outbuildings survive.

A VIEW OF MALLER'S SMALL NURSERY in the angle of Upwood Road and Leyland Road, Lee, in the 1890s. (His main fields were in the area now bisected by Westhorne Avenue.) The houses on the left were Nos 2 to 12 Dorville Road; No. 6 was then the home of the novelist Jeffrey Farnol. The Maller family lived at No. 72 Leyland Road, the house with the conservatory. See p. 32 for their shop.

A HAYMAKING SCENE AT CROFTON PARK, probably c. 1910. The field was opposite St Hilda's church, and is now largely covered by Otford Crescent and the houses on the south side of Sevenoaks Road, although part of it remains open as a sports ground. This small farm belonged to the Noakes family, the brewers, who lived just to the north at Brockley Hall.

On the River

THE MOUTH OF THE RAVENSBOURNE, otherwise known as Deptford Creek, in 1898.

THIS EVOCATIVE PHOTOGRAPH of the River Ravensbourne near Ladywell was taken by Henry Wood in the late 1850s.

THE WOOD FAMILY MOVED TO BROOK-
LANDS, a house built in 1782 or a
little later, in 1859. It is now a
musical instruments shop, No.
272 Lewisham High Street. Like
their old home Sion House,
Brooklands had a large garden
running back to the Ravensbourne, and it was here in 1859 or
1860 that Henry Wood took these
two views. Much of this area is now
occupied by the Lewisham
Council depot in Wearside Road.

HENRY WOOD TOOK THIS PHOTOGRAPH of Ladywell Bridge only a year or two after the houses on the right (now Nos 51 and 53 Ladywell Road) were built in 1857. In the foreground is the footpath which still runs through St Mary's churchyard to Lewisham High Street.

THE QUAGGY RIVER, which is the main tributary of the Ravensbourne, has often proved a troublesome neighbour to the people of Lee. One of the worst of its many floods occurred in April 1878, when much property was damaged, including the bridge in Eastdown Park (above). These scenes were captured by the prolific postcard publisher William Perkins, to whom we are indebted for many illustrations in this volume. The picture below was a particularly poignant one for him. It shows his own garden at No. 10 Weardale Road, with the houses of Eastdown Park beyond.

DURING THE LONG EDWARDIAN SUMMER a passion for boating gripped those residents of Catford Hill whose gardens ran down to the Ravensbourne. Many had their own landing stages. Here George Wells of Clovelly, No. 33 Catford Hill, flirts with Cissie Duffin, who lived at Heathfield, No. 37. The view is upstream, towards the confluence of the Pool River and the Ravensbourne. Clovelly and Heathfield are now shops. Various other members of the 'club' appear in the lower photograph opposite. They are, back row, left to right: Mr Offlow, George Wells, Fred Wells, Albert Wells, -?-. Front row: Jack Stanford, Harry Roberts, Harry Reader. Behind the fort: Vane Stobbs. The Stanfords lived at Deepdene, No. 43, the Stobbs family at Northbrook, No. 47, and the Readers at Fernbank, No. 35. Mr Offlow was probably Arthur Roland Offlow of No. 30 Berlin Road, now Canadian Avenue.

IN THE PHOTOGRAPH ABOVE, Fred Wells of Clovelly is seen relaxing by his own landing stage. In the background is the railway viaduct running up to Catford station. The boating enthusiasts held an annual regatta, which included some alfresco amateur dramatics. The subject was usually bloodthirsty – cowboys and indians, or cannibals – but the entertainment shown below, c. 1908, apparently had a patriotic theme. For the identifications see p. 24.

IN THE SUMMER OF 1898 these three simian schoolboys made a pilgrimage down the Ravensbourne from its rise at Keston to its junction with the Thames at Deptford, taking with them a friendly photographer to record the journey in detail. The view on the left, taken at Bellingham, they captioned 'after the tiddlers'. The one below, called 'once a good swim', shows the Ravensbourne at Southend. I wish I had room for all of this charming series; other examples appear on pp. 19, 105 and 108.

SECTION THREE

Street Scene

LEWISHAM HIGH STREET, C. 1916, showing the post office which was destroyed in 1944.

ALBURY STREET, DEPTFORD was planned and largely built between 1705 and 1717 by Thomas Lucas, who died in the High Street in 1736. He named his development Union Street, after the parliamentary union with Scotland in 1707. (It only became Albury Street in 1898.) Lucas was the master bricklayer employed on St Paul's, Deptford (see p. 66), and also on a number of Hawksmoor's finest churches. The road was largely intact when this view was taken, c. 1900, but bureaucratic bungling has allowed it to decay badly since the Second World War, and now only a few of these fine houses survive.

High Street, Deptford

THE SOUTHERN END OF DEPTFORD HIGH STREET viewed from the Broadway, c. 1905. On the right is the High Street branch of Peppercorn's (see pp. 129 and 131) at No. 14. The bow-windowed houses on either side, both converted into shops, are reminders that this was a good residential street in the eighteenth century. The one on the left (No. 13), then Lipton's, survives as the Vision Hire shop.

THE VIEW EASTWARDS OVER NEW CROSS GATE, and along New Cross Road, from the roof of The White Hart, c. 1903. (For the reverse view see p. 53.) Thomas Francott's tobacconist's shop was at No. 193 New Cross Road. The London and South Western Bank is now Barclays.

LEWISHAM HIGH ROAD, now Lewisham Way, c. 1910. St John's church (seen also on p. 31) was built in 1854/5, architect P.C. Hardwick. On the left is No. 287 Lewisham Way, which dates from 1868.

A HORSE BUS LABOURING UP LOAMPIT HILL, c. 1903. On the right is the spire of St John's, with the church hall below. Slightly nearer is the booking hall of Lewisham Road station, on the Greenwich Park line, which closed in 1917. The building still survives. The shops on the left, Nos 55 to 59, had just been built.

THE ST JOHN'S DISTRICT, the meeting place of Lewisham, Deptford, and Brockley, in the mid-1920s. In its early days St John's might have been described as the Janus church. At the front it looked out on the smiling prosperity of Brockley, exemplified in Breakspears Road (bottom left), and Tressillian Road, crossing the railway bridge in the foreground. At the back St John's confronted the poverty of Deptford New Town, and the appalling slums of Brookmill Road, which is almost touched by the church spire in this picture. The Greenwich Park railway line, which cuts through the centre, had been closed for nearly a decade by this time. In the top left-hand corner are the derelict Blackheath Hill station, and the distinctive double spire of Holy Trinity church. Top right are Morden Hill and the edge of Blackheath.

LEWISHAM HIGH STREET in the 1870s, showing the lamp standard which was replaced by the clock tower in 1897. These shops, known as Granville Terrace, or The High Pavement, were built in 1853. The Army and Navy store and Tower House now occupy the site. Note the shop of Benjamin Maller, fruiterer and seedsman, part of whose nursery can be seen on p. 17.

AN 1876 VIEW OF THE AREA now occupied by the northern half of the Lewisham High Street market. Marks and Spencer's is now on the site of most of the buildings on the left, including Henry Wheeler's sweet shop. The four men on the right are outside The Albion pub at the corner of Lewis Grove. (See also pp. 140, 141 and 156.)

THE HOSPITALS WELFARE SOCIETY organized a number of fund-raising fêtes at Perry's Upper Mill Farm, Southend, in fields now covered by Winlaton Road, etc. in the early 1920s. They were preceded by fancy dress parades down Lewisham High Street. This one is just passing Ladywell Park (see p. 34).

THE VIEW SOUTHWARDS ALONG LEWISHAM HIGH STREET from the street market, c. 1930. On the right is one of Lewisham's lost pubs, The White Hart; on the left the just completed Catholic church, with its striking campanile.

LADYWELL in the mid-1920s. In the right foreground is Ladywell station, with Ladywell Fields beyond. Curving away from the station to meet Lewisham High Street left centre is Ladywell Road. On the opposite side of the High Street notice the tree-lined Ladywell Park, a road which no longer exists. It was badly bombed during the Second World War, and subsequently cleared to make way for the new swimming baths. St Mary's church is prominent in the centre of the photograph. Above it is Romborough Way, then newly built on old allotments, as the council's first 'homes-for-heroes' housing development. Beyond it, at the extreme top of the picture, are the grounds of Camps Hill House, now the site of the Hether Grove Estate. Top right is part of Lewisham Park, then still a private amenity for the occupants of the encircling houses.

THE LEWISHAM END OF LEE HIGH ROAD viewed from the Belmont Hill and Lewis Grove crossroads, c. 1904. On the right is The Sultan, which then had a greengrocer's shop (now incorporated with the pub) between it and Clarendon Rise.

MANOR PARK, LEE, looking north, with the corner of Staplehurst Road on the left. The scene is little changed today. This postcard was sent on 11 August 1914, at the end of a momentous week. Maude told her friend Winnie (forgetting her spelling in her agitation): 'we are very quite at buisness we have started our holiday's this week instead of next. I expect it is owing to the war, nearly every buisness place is the same.'

Lee Green, S.E.

LEE HIGH ROAD FROM LEE GREEN, c. 1900. The Lee Green fire station was established here c. 1895, and replaced by the present building in Eltham Road in 1906. Opposite are Lee police station and the Prince Arthur beershop. Whittle and Leslie were bootmakers.

Burnt Ash Road, Lee.

THE LEE GREEN END OF BURNT ASH ROAD in 1902, showing the area now occupied by Sainsbury's supermarket. The shops were William Brown, coal, corn, and flour merchant; J. Morgan, greengrocer; Walbank Teasdale, stationer (and postmaster); and George Gooding, draper and milliner.

MOUNT PLEASANT ROAD, looking west towards Lewisham High Street c. 1910, when the roads were safe for dogs and children. The houses were built in the 1870s.

HITHER GREEN LANE at 1.45 p.m. on 11 July 1910. The view is north-westwards from Torridon Road. The shops on the left, then Nos 216 to 246, later 246 to 274, were known as the Central Market. Skipping is no longer recommended in the middle of Hither Green Lane at any hour.

THE VIEW WESTWARDS ALONG GEORGE LANE from the entrance to Radford Road, c. 1910. George Lane was an old farm track in which a number of houses – most still surviving – were built behind the George Inn c. 1815. But at this eastern end development was not quite complete in 1910, and the road was still unmade.

BROWNHILL ROAD, looking west from the corner of Laleham Road, c. 1905. On the right is No. 115, the corner grocery of Frederick John Staines. In the middle of the picture are two houses (Nos 103 and 105) being converted into shops, an everyday event at that period, but one not often captured in photographs.

CATFORD HILL in the 1870s. The view is north-east towards Catford Bridge. The finger-post points into Stanstead Road; the ivy-clad building behind it is the Ravensbourne Tavern (see p. 60). The tall houses on either side of Stanstead Road, then known as Elm Villas, survive as shops. The nearer pair are now Nos 28 and 30 Catford Hill. The building opposite the Ravensbourne was the Ship, a long-vanished and forgotten beerhouse. The peaceful-looking white gate in the foreground marked the entrance to a footpath, which is now enlarged as the second branch of Stanstead Road, and the vital element in the one-way system at this busy junction on the South Circular.

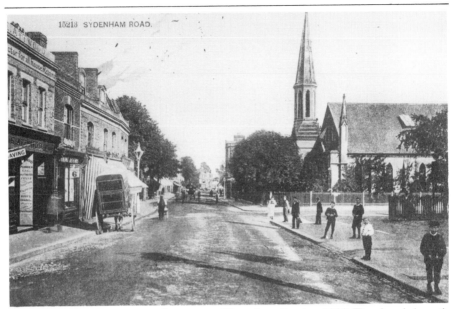

SYDENHAM ROAD, looking east to the corner of Trewsbury Road, c. 1900. The church (now the hall of All Saints', Trewsbury Road) has had a complicated history. It was built as a dissenting chapel in the mid-eighteenth century, but has since oscillated between the Anglicans and the NonConformists in bewildering style. The spire (now lost) was added in 1845.

CHAPLIN STREET, FOREST HILL, which ran between Church Vale and Hindsley Place, was a development of the 1850s. This view of the east side was taken in 1938, shortly before it was demolished as part of a slum clearance programme. The corner shop (No. 1) was then run by Frederick Dalgleish.

SECTION FOUR

Homes of the Rich and Poor

THE CEDARS, BELMONT HILL, LEE, while in use as a military hospital, c. 1917.

TWO UNFAMILIAR VIEWS OF THE LIMES, Lewisham High Street: above, the garden front, and below, the hall. This house was noted for its connection with John and Charles Wesley and George Whitefield, who were all friendly with various of its occupants. Between the 1730s and 1782 John Wesley frequently rested here between preaching tours, first as the guest of Mrs Jane Sparrow, and later with the banker Ebenezer Blackwell, who acted as the Methodist leader's financial adviser. The Limes was demolished in 1894. Its site is now occupied by Nos 155 to 171 Lewisham High Street.

THIS VIEW OF LEWISHAM HIGH STREET in the 1880s shows Lewisham House, which stood on the southern corner of Ladywell Road until 1893. It was an Elizabethan building, remodelled in 1680 by Sir John Lethieullier and his wife Anne. She was the daughter of Sir William Hooker, Lord Mayor of London, and had the not very exclusive distinction of being admired by Samuel Pepys. In the nineteenth century Lewisham House was owned by the Parkers, the town's leading solicitors. The last of the line was George Parker, 'a rich recluse who was the poor man's lawyer. You wrote your problem and put it in a hole in the wall; in 24 hours the answer was put there. You never saw him.' On the right of the photograph is The Black Bull, now sadly renamed The Fox and Firkin.

DACRE HOUSE was built in Church Lane, Lee (now Brandram Road) in 1724, or a year or two earlier. Notable occupants included Sir Samuel Fludyer (1705–68), Lord Mayor of London, John Carnac (1716–1800) and Harry Verelst (1735–85), two nabobs, and the eighteenth Baron Dacre of the South, who married Sir Samuel Fludyer's niece. The original house had two delicate single-storey wings, but in the early 1850s these were raised to the height of the main block, and the house was divided into three dwellings, the centre section with eight bedrooms, the wings with ten each. This picture shows the garden front of the southern third, probably c. 1880, when the tenant was John Standring, a wine merchant. The bay window was a survival from the original 1720s wing. Dacre House was demolished c. 1897.

THE EARLS OF DARTMOUTH, Lords of the Manor of Lewisham, lived at Dartmouth House, Dartmouth Row, Blackheath (which was rebuilt in its present form c. 1750), fairly regularly during the eighteenth century, but later it was used by minor members of the family. This photograph shows the library during the tenancy, c. 1893 to 1905, of Huyshe Wolcot Yeatman-Biggs, Bishop of Southwark, who had married the earl's daughter.

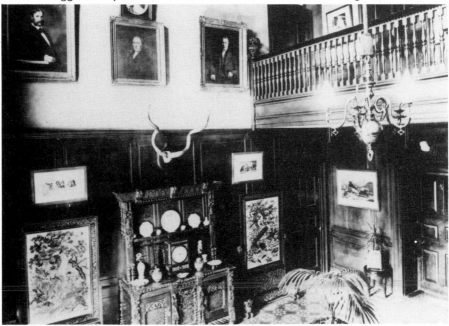

THE HALL OF PENTLAND HOUSE, Old Road, Lee, during the occupancy of the Whyte family, between the late 1870s and 1911. Since then it has been a Goldsmiths' College hall of residence. The house, which was built in the 1680s, is one of the oldest remaining in Lewisham.

NOS 1 TO 41 LEWISHAM HILL were built c. 1820, and originally called Dartmouth Terrace. They formed an attractive feature opposite Colfe's school until 17 June 1944, when a flying bomb destroyed the school and many of the houses. Blocks of flats now occupy the whole site.

CUTHBERT WILKINSON AND HIS FAMILY on the garden steps of their home, Florian, in Lawrie Park Avenue, Sydenham, during the 1890s. The house (originally called St Germains) was built c. 1861, and demolished in the early 1950s. Nos 23 to 27 occupy the site.

LEE LODGE IN LEE HIGH ROAD was built in 1827, and originally called The Thatched House. This photograph probably shows the Smallman family, the occupants from 1890 to 1893. The house was demolished c. 1895, when Manor Park Parade was built on the frontage.

THE SPARE ROOM AND BATHROOM OF THE HOLLIES, Lewisham, in September 1910, when it was the home of the Karlowa family. The Hollies, built in the late 1860s, stood in a large garden at the end of Romer Avenue, and survived when the rest of the road was replaced by the Lewisham Shopping Centre. It still exists in Molesworth Street, though probably not for much longer.

SIR GEORGE GROVE (1820–1900) lived for forty years in a seventeenth-century wooden house in Sydenham Road. This is his study, in which he wrote his *Dictionary of Music and Musicians*. The house was demolished in 1929, and the site is now occupied by the presbytery of the church of Our Lady and St Philip Neri.

THESE LONG-DEMOLISHED COTTAGES in Midway Place (the area behind the Old Manor House pub in Bush Road, Deptford) were built by the Revd Thomas Beck, a Methodist, in the garden of the house in which he lived from 1788 to 1844. The lady in the doorway was Beck's granddaughter Dora Kingsford.

BULL'S EYE COTTAGE, which stood at the corner of Fordyce Road in Hither Green Lane, was the gardener's house to The Laurels, a villa a little further south, opposite Mountsfield Court. It was better known as Japes's Cottage, after the family of hereditary gardeners who occupied it from the 1840s until its demolition in the 1880s.

THESE ANCIENT COTTAGES, which faced the lower mill pond (now the Homebase pond) at Southend village, were demolished c. 1870. The woman in the doorway was probably the wife of Henry Cox, the carpenter who lived here for many years. The cottage, part of which appears on the right, was the childhood home of H.C. Mott, author of the truly appalling poem 'My Native Place: on leaving the Hamlet of Southend in August 1869'. On the left can be glimpsed Southend chapel, now the hall of St John's church.

NO, NOT BARNSLEY, but the prosperous London suburb of Lee. Dacre Square lay off the south side of Dacre Street, later Fludyer Street. This was the heart of Lee New Town, a working-class enclave built in the 1820s and '30s over the gardens of Lee Place, the moated mansion of the Boone family (see p. 51). Dacre Square was removed as part of a slum clearance programme shortly after this photograph was taken, c. 1935, and almost all of Lee New Town has followed it into oblivion. Some was destroyed by bombing during the Second World War, and much more was demolished in the 1950s to make way for a council estate.

THESE ALMSHOUSES IN LEE HIGH ROAD were built in 1683 by Christopher Boone of Lee Place, an ancestor of the American explorer Daniel Boone. The photograph was taken shortly before they were demolished in 1875, when a new set of Boone's Almshouses was opened nearer Lee Green. The delightful chapel was retained, however, and still graces the High Road.

SAYES COURT, the Deptford home of John Evelyn (and also for a time of Peter the Great), was demolished in the 1720s, and its materials probably used in the building of a workhouse on the site. When this photograph was taken, c. 1900, it had been converted into almshouses for the Evelyn family's old retainers. The building was demolished in the 1930s.

THE ST OLAVE'S POOR LAW UNION, a grouping of five parishes in Southwark, Bermondsey, and Rotherhithe, could not provide enough workhouse accommodation within its own crowded streets, so in 1900 it opened a huge new institution for its 'aged and infirm poor' on Slagrave Farm at Ladywell (see pp. 11 and 143). Here they are at dinner. It looks grim enough, but was regarded at the time as unusually humane. Later the building was taken over by the London County Council as an old people's home called Ladywell Lodge, but has now been largely demolished.

THIS SECTION REALLY DOES TAKE US from the rich man in his castle to the poor man at his gate, because this late nineteenth-century gipsy encampment was in the grounds of The Cedars, Belmont Hill (see p. 41), the home of the Penn family. The roadway behind the caravans was probably Love Lane, now Heath Lane.

SECTION FIVE

Public Houses

THE WHITE HART at New Cross Gate, c. 1900.

THE FIVE BELLS, New Cross Road, in the 1920s. It was an ancient inn, rebuilt in its present handsome style in 1841. The turning at the side, now Hatcham Park Road, was previously known as Five Bells Lane.

THE BROCKLEY JACK must have been one of the most photographed and painted inns in London, but this view is unusual in setting it in context in a quite undeveloped Brockley Road. Its name is comparatively recent. In the eighteenth century it was called The Crooked Billet, and for much of the nineteenth, The Castle. The Jack was rebuilt in its present form in 1898. John Noakes, the brewer, lived across the road at Brockley Hall.

THE MAID OF THE MILL in Mill Road, Lewisham, during the 1920s. It was established as a beerhouse in a pair of early nineteenth-century cottages – part of a group known as Stratford Place – in the 1850s, and demolished in 1964. See also p. 102.

THE DUKE OF CAMBRIDGE on the northern corner of Lewisham High Street and Loampit Vale, c. 1905. It had been founded in a small cottage during the 1840s, and rebuilt as shown here c. 1880. The third and last pub replaced it in 1929, but was itself swept away by a traffic scheme in 1992.

THE TIGER'S HEAD AT LEE GREEN, which has been known as The Old Tiger's Head since the nineteenth century to distinguish it from its upstart rival across the road, was built in the 1730s on a part of the village green, and rebuilt in 1896. The original inn is shown in the photograph above, the present one in the view below, taken in June 1902. The verses, which those of a sensitive disposition are advised not to read, celebrate Edward VII's recovery from appendicitis.

THE CASTLE, LEWISHAM HIGH STREET, in the 1880s, when Edward Mount was the landlord. A house on this site was bequeathed to the parish in 1630, but the inn was probably not founded until the second half of the eighteenth century. It has since been rebuilt, but retains its old name and site. On the left, at the corner of Hither Green Lane, which then ran down to the High Street, is the shop of the versatile Robert Patch, grocer, wine merchant, postmaster, and assistant registrar.

THE ELM TREE BEERHOUSE in Rushey Green photographed, probably by Henry Wood, in the late 1850s. It was one of a group of cottages built on wasteland on the east side of the road in the eighteenth century. It was demolished c. 1870. The shops on the southern corner of Honley Road now occupy the site.

AN OUTING ABOUT TO START from The Plough and Harrow, Rushey Green, c. 1906. The pub, which was established in the early 1850s, in an older cottage, is not much altered today. The tall shop to the right was the off-licence.

THE BLACK HORSE, or Black Horse and Harrow, Rushey Green in 1876, when the landlord was William Bray. This pub, which was founded before 1700, has been rebuilt at least twice, the last time in 1897. The house on the left, behind the flagpole, was the Catford police station (see p. 112).

THE RAVENSBOURNE TAVERN, Catford Hill (see also p. 39) in the late nineteenth century. The pub, which was first licensed in 1845, was rebuilt c. 1900, and has now been renamed The Prince Henry.

THE OLD TWO BREWERS at Perry Hill appeared to be an early eighteenth-century house, but did not become an inn until late in the century. The photograph shows it when the publican had established a bicycle business as a sideline, probably in the late 1880s. The Two Brewers was rebuilt in its present form in 1926.

THE CHANGES TO THE GREEN MAN at Southend village faithfully mirrored those in the area as a whole. In the 1850s (above) it was a quiet village inn, but the increasing population of Lewisham brought an influx of pleasure-seekers, and to accommodate them The Green Man was rebuilt on a larger scale c. 1860. It was not big enough, though, to cope with the huge crowds who invaded Southend in the 1920s, by tram, or on foot from the new estates of Bellingham and Downham, so the pub was entirely rebuilt again as seen below. The old mill pond was also adapted to the new conditions as a boating lake known as Peter Pan's (now the Homebase) Pool.

THIS EARLY TWENTIETH-CENTURY GROUP at the Greyhound Hotel in Kirkdale, Sydenham, was the local motor cycle club preparing for an outing. The Greyhound, which was founded c. 1720, is Sydenham's oldest inn. It is now dominated by a large Victorian extension, but the rear of the building is considerably older, as were the stables, on the right of the picture, which have now been swept away.

THE SWISS COTTAGE IN STANSTEAD ROAD, Forest Hill (seen here c. 1900), was one of Lewisham's most distinctive pubs. It was built in the early 1850s, and operated as a beerhouse until granted a full licence in 1854. In recent years it was burdened with the unfortunate new name of 'Tyrols'. The Swiss Cottage was demolished in 1990.

Houses of God

THE CHURCH OF THE ASCENSION, Dartmouth Row, Blackheath, c. 1900.

LEWISHAM'S ANCIENT PARISH CHURCH OF ST MARY'S, C. 1900. It had been rebuilt between 1774 and 1777 by George Gibson, the town's finest architect. The intriguing 'men only' lectures were given in the parish hall in Ladywell Road. One of the advertised speakers was the writer G.W.E. Russell. On the left is Church House (demolished in 1907) which in the eighteenth century had doubled as a butcher's shop and inn under the sign of The Bull.

THE CLERGY AND CHOIR OF ST MARY'S in 1907, when they mustered in numbers that many a modern vicar would be glad to see in his congregation. The Revd William Woodcock Hough, later Bishop of Woolwich (seated in the centre of the second row from the back), was the Vicar of Lewisham at the time.

THE LYCH-GATE OF ST MARGARET'S was built in 1882 as a memorial to Lady Adelaide Law, wife of Frederick Law, rector from 1873 to 1900. This early twentieth-century postcard shows its original position at the corner of Lee Terrace and Brandram Road. It was moved to the Church Terrace entrance in 1957.

THE ARCHITECTURAL GLORY OF DEPTFORD is St Paul's church in the High Street. It was designed by Thomas Archer in 1713, as one of Queen Anne's thanksgiving churches, but not completed until 1730. This 1893 view of the west end shows the graveyard before the tombstones were removed.

ST CATHERINE'S IN PEPYS ROAD, New Cross, has had a short but eventful life. It was built in 1894. In 1913 it was severely damaged by fire, a disaster for which the suffragettes were universally blamed, though without any proof. The photograph shows the extent of the destruction. The church was repaired in 1914, only to be wrecked by bombing in 1940. It was restored again in 1950.

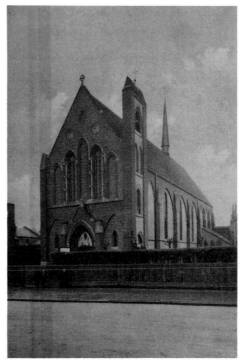

THE ROMAN CATHOLIC CHURCH OF OUR LADY AND ST PHILIP NERI in Sydenham Road was built in 1882, at the corner of Watlington Grove, a site now occupied by the houses numbered 192 to 206. This postcard shows it c. 1900. It was destroyed by bombing in 1940, and re-built on its present site in 1959.

THE LONDON ORATORY at Brompton was founded by the poet Father Frederick Faber (1814–63) in 1849. One of his original confrères was Father John Bowden, his eventual successor and biographer. The Bowden family owned 10 acres of land on Sydenham Hill, and they gave this to the oratory as the site of a country house for the recreation of the fathers. It was built in 1852, and called St Mary's. The house was compulsorily purchased by the London County Council in 1951, and demolished to make way for the Sydenham Hill Estate.

THE OPENING OF THE REBUILT SOUTH LEE TABERNACLE, Baring Road, in 1911. The first church had been opened in 1874 as the Bromley Road Tabernacle, that being the old name for Baring Road. It became the South Lee Baptist church in 1934, and is now the South Lee Christian Centre. The road at the side of the church (on the left of the picture) was called Butterfield Street in 1911, but is now Waite Davies Road, in honour of James Waite Davies, the minister of the tabernacle from 1886 to 1930. He is the grey-bearded man standing inside the railings, a little to the left of the notice-board.

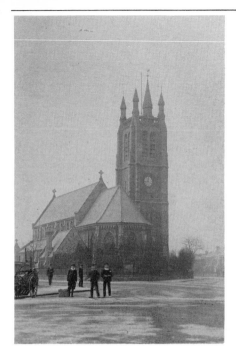

AMONG THE BEST of the borough's Victorian churches is St George's, Perry Hill, which was built between 1878 and 1880, to a design by W.C. Banks of Lewisham. It was paid for by George Parker of Lewisham House (see p. 43). Its individualizing touch, the one larger pinnacle, was an afterthought of Parker's. The clock was given by his niece and heiress, the happily-named Miss Rich.

THE OBOS ('others before ourselves') club of St Augustine's, Grove Park, seeing in the new year of 1945. The members were, back row, left to right: Mr Squires, Ken Groves, the Revd F.O. Burt (vicar 1942–56). Front row: -?-, Geoff Bawcutt, Mrs Ivy Tollitt.

Sports and Customs

CRICKET AT THE CATFORD CYCLING TRACK (see p. 75) in the 1890s.

A JACK-IN-THE-GREEN TROUPE in Lewisham High Street, nearly opposite Ladywell Road, in 1903. The Jack was hidden in the wickerwork frame covered with leaves and flowers. His attendants, all male despite the costumes, were collecting pennies. J.G. Frazer and others have regarded Jack-in-the-Green as a survival of pagan rites, but as a chimney sweeps' May-Day custom it is not recorded in this form before 1800. (Compare this photograph with one on p. 33.)

THE PARTY WHICH CARRIED OUT THE ANCIENT CUSTOM of beating the bounds of Lewisham in May 1897. It took them three days to complete the circuit.

THE LEWISHAM RIFLE CLUB RANGE at Holloway Farm, Southend, was opened on 27 April 1901, amid the excitement and anxieties of the Boer War. It survived long enough to train a generation of Lewisham marksmen for the First World War, but disappeared under the Downham Estate in the 1920s. The site of the longest firing position, 600 yards, is now occupied by No. 500 Bromley Road; the target by the grounds of the Rangefield schools. The Mayor of Lewisham fired the first shot, and missed the target completely. He was Theophilus William Williams (seated front centre in this photograph of the event), an extraordinary suburban Lloyd George, who dominated Lewisham politics from the 1870s until the beginning of the twentieth century. Behind a façade of respectability and piety this Congregational lay preacher lived an extravagant life financed by fraud and embezzlement. He was finally exposed in 1908, and after a dramatic arrest at Liverpool Street had foiled his planned escape to France, he gave his creditors the slip by taking an overdose of morphia. (For another glimpse of Theophilus Williams see p. 96.)

THE BLACKHEATH GOLF CLUB is the oldest in England, with a documented history from the middle of the eighteenth century. Its five-hole course, later extended to seven, used the numerous gravel pits and ponds of Blackheath as its hazards. This photograph shows a match played on 24 March 1893. The man driving was J.G. Gibson. Play became difficult as Blackheath grew busier, and when the army requisitioned the heath in 1914, and the golfers had to take refuge at the Eltham course, they soon decided to stay. The Blackheath and Eltham golf clubs joined forces in 1923.

THE CATFORD CYCLING CLUB was founded in 1886, and rose rapidly to European prominence. The photograph above shows the Kittens' first evening race meeting, at Mayow Park, Sydenham, on 28 June 1887. In 1894 they built their own track (below) south of Brownhill Road, and for a few years attracted huge crowds to their meetings, at which the top professionals raced. But the coming of the motor car ended the cycling boom, and in 1900 the track was closed, and soon built over. Only F.W. Reed's grandstand, 'with a suggestion of Japanese art in its lines', survives as a warehouse in Sportsbank Street, and that has been shorn of its pagoda roof since 1983. The club continued after the loss of its track, and is still flourishing. (See also p. 71.)

THE LEWISHAM CRICKET GROUND, which lay north of Ladywell Road, in fields now covered by the southern ends of Algernon Road and Embleton Road, was the local home of the great game from 1864 until the land was required for building in the 1880s. The photograph above, taken in 1870 from what is now Hilly Fields, gives a general view of the ground. The lower picture was taken (at much the same date) from the steps of the pavilion in the centre of the view above. The photographer was a professional, Robert Hatt of No. 16 Surrey Terrace, Counter Hill, now No. 100 Lewisham Way. The event was probably one of the athletic sports days of the Lewisham Cricket Club, which tended to be 'numerously and fashionably attended, carriages extending half way round the enclosure'.

THE OLD PAVILION of the Private Banks Cricket Ground at Catford in 1876, a couple of years after it was opened. County cricket was first played here in June 1875, when Lord Harris hit ninety-two in Kent's crushing defeat of Hampshire. The other star was a local hero, Frank Penn of The Cedars (see p. 41). But 'notwithstanding the beauty of the ground and the unvarying excellence of the wickets, the attendance at Catford Bridge in this match was still meagre'. Kent only began to play regularly at Catford in the 1890s.

CRICKET HAS BEEN PLAYED ON BLACKHEATH since at least the 1820s, though it is hard to imagine that nervous batsmen have ever regarded its wiry turf with enthusiasm. By 1890 the London County Council was maintaining thirty-six pitches, and this view of the area north of All Saints' church shows how well they were used.

THE SWIMMING POOL at Goldsmiths' College, New Cross, seen here c. 1906, was built by the Goldsmiths' Company during the 1890s. It was badly damaged by bombing in 1940, and totally destroyed by fire in May 1945.

BELLINGHAM OPEN AIR BATHS, seen here shortly after they were opened in 1922, occupied a site between the Ravensbourne and the railway line, just south of the junction of Randlesdown Road (which can be seen in the distance on the left) and Bromley Road (seen on the right). The pool closed some years ago and the site has now been redeveloped.

LEWISHAM SWIMMING CLUB'S much-capped water polo team in 1911. Back row, left to right: A.H. Atkins, G.F.N. Wilkinson, G.W. Ingersoll, -?-. Front row: H.S. Coppock, R. Shove, A.R. Ingersoll, J.W. Stafford, -?-. The original photograph has been damaged by water.

DURING THE GALA HELD AT DOWNHAM BATHS on 2 September 1950, as part of the celebration of the Borough of Lewisham's fiftieth anniversary (see also p. 147), the Croydon Mannequin Academy staged this parade of seventy-five years of bathing fashions.

A CATFORD SKATING CLUB GYMKHANA at The Rink (see p. 126), c. 1912. They look serious enough, but the contests on these occasions included such things as a 'ginger beer and bun race for gentlemen amateurs'.

A CHARACTERISTIC PIECE OF ACTION during the friendly match between Deptford civil defence and police teams played at Millwall's ground, the Den, on 26 March 1942.

SECTION EIGHT

Transport

CATFORD BRIDGE STATION, probably in the 1870s.

THE BROMLEY COACH OUTSIDE THE GEORGE, at the northern end of Rushey Green, c. 1870. There were still plenty of regular coach services at this period, carrying commuters on the routes not yet taken over by the railways; but the rather raffish crowd on this vehicle look as if they were on a pleasure trip, perhaps to the races. The George had been established in some old farm buildings on this site in the second half of the eighteenth century, and was rebuilt c. 1800. It has been much restored in recent decades, but is still basically unaltered. Only the stables have been removed. There was an earlier George in the High Street, where the library car park is now, but whether there was any connection between the two establishments is doubtful.

AT THE BEGINNING OF THE EIGHTEENTH CENTURY many turnpike trusts were established to improve the country's main roads. The local trustees raised money by a toll upon road users, collected at strategically placed gates: a penny for a horse, twopence for a carriage, sixpence for a waggon, etc. The authority for this area was the New Cross Turnpike Trust, established in 1718. The two of its gates shown here, with the toll collectors' cottages beside them, were the New Cross Gate (above), at the junction with Queen's Road, and the Lee Green Gate (below), by Cambridge Drive in Eltham Road. The pub behind the New Cross gate was The White Hart (see p. 53). The turnpikes became very unpopular in the nineteenth century, and were abolished one by one by the New Cross Trust in 1865.

THOMAS TILLING, A FARMER'S SON, started his transport empire in Peckham in 1851 with a single horse-bus, and the firm quickly expanded in all directions. A feature of his buses, the fine pairs of greys which often pulled them, is illustrated by the Brockley Bus (above), a New Cross to Lower Sydenham service seen in Brockley Road, just passing St Margaret's Road. The firm needed a great number of stables for all its horses. It acquired the yard below, next to the Manor House Gardens in Old Road, Lee, in 1901, and retained it until 1928, for the last fifteen years as a motor coach factory. The cobbled entrance is little changed today.

LEWISHAM ROAD STATION, at the top of Loampit Hill, c. 1900. This was the view north-westwards towards Blackheath. The station opened in 1871, as part of the Greenwich Park branch, and closed in 1917. Most of the line has been dismantled, but this section was linked to Lewisham station by a loop line in 1929. The old booking hall and stationmaster's house survive, the latter in Whidborne Close. (See also pp. 30 and 31.)

THIS LOOKS LIKE A SCENE FROM A MOTORIST'S NIGHTMARE, but was a common sight in Grove Street, Deptford, where a spur from the Deptford Wharf branch ran down the middle of the road to the foreign cattle market and its successors (see p. 107). The photograph was taken c. 1948, when the Evelyn Arms at the corner of Windmill Lane was in ruins after bomb damage.

THE PARKES'S BRIDGE SIGNAL BOX between St John's and Hither Green stations, c. 1910. (For Parkes see p. 103.) The four large dials were Walker's rotary train describers, an important South Eastern Railway contribution to signalling technology.

NEW CROSS TRAM DEPOT was opened in 1906. It was built on the site of Fairlawn, an eighteenth-century house long occupied by the Edmonds family, leading market gardeners in the area. The flats on the right in the picture above are known as Fairlawn Mansions. The South-East London District Synagogue, on the left, was opened in 1904. The tram depot was the largest in London, housing 326 tram-cars, some of which are seen below. It is now the New Cross bus garage.

AN ELECTRIC AND A HORSE TRAM TOGETHER at The Black Horse, Rushey Green, in 1907. The archway led into the horse tram depot, later Timpson's garage (see p. 89). James Webb and Sons were flour merchants who occupied part of the tram yard.

INFLATION IS A DISEASE OF LANGUAGES as much as of economies. Only one passenger was killed in this 'disaster' on 2 September 1911, when a trainee tram driver tried to take the turn from Shardeloes Road into Lewisham Way too fast, and was derailed.

THE OLD HORSE TRAM DEPOT at No. 175 Rushey Green (see p. 88) was the headquarters of Alexander Timpson and Son, the bus and coach operators, from 1920 to 1974, and was then occupied until quite recently by National Travel Ltd. This photograph shows Timpson's fleet of charabancs at Rushey Green in 1927.

THE ROYAL ARSENAL CO-OPERATIVE SOCIETY had its own fleet of charabancs, which in this photograph of c. 1920 are about to set off on an outing from the Deptford Co-op at Nos 8 to 12 High Street.

TWO BUS CONDUCTRESSES during the First World War, when the clippies made their debut. The 75 still plied the same route from Croydon to Woolwich via Catford and Lee, though probably much more slowly in modern traffic, until 1991.

THE GREAT AIRSHIP PIONEER in the UK was the Welshman E.T. Willows. On the night of 7 and 8 August 1910 he established a long-distance record by flying the ship he had designed and built himself, the Willows II, from Cardiff to London. He intended to land at the Crystal Palace, then the Mecca of British aviators, but overshot and came to earth at Melrose Farm, Winn Road, Lee. The farmer, John Money Woodman, appropriately made the most of the situation by charging the many sightseers sixpence for admission.

Seats of Learning

ST DUNSTAN'S COLLEGE, Stanstead Road, Catford, c. 1905.

LEWISHAM'S OLDEST SCHOOL is no longer in Lewisham. Colfe's grammar school was founded by Abraham Colfe, the vicar, in 1652, and rebuilt on its original site in Lewisham Hill in 1889. The photograph shows it shortly afterwards, with Walerand Road at its side. The school was destroyed by a flying bomb on 17 June 1944, and in 1964 Colfe's moved to a new home at Horn Park, a few yards over the border into Greenwich.

STANHOPE'S SCHOOL IN DEPTFORD HIGH STREET was built in 1723 by George Stanhope, vicar of Deptford and Lewisham, and demolished in 1882. The site is now occupied by Nos 70 and 72. Its endowment was subsequently combined with another charity to finance the Addey and Stanhope school in New Cross Road. The statue of the charity girl is preserved there.

THE REVD JOHN WOOD TODD, the first minister of the Baptist church in Dartmouth Road, with some of the pupils of his 'select establishment for young ladies' at Tudor Hall, South Road, Forest Hill, c. 1880. The school had been founded by Todd and his wife in the early 1850s at Perry Hill House, and moved to Tudor Hall c. 1865. After Todd's death the school was taken over by his son-in-law John Hamilton, later a judge and the first Lord Sumner. So Maude Todd, one of the ugliest women in England, ended her days as a viscountess, which sounds like a story with a moral. Only the wing of the house to the right still survives. The main block was demolished in the 1950s. Lord Sumner is commemorated by the Hamilton Hall, which stands on the site of the stables.

EDGEHILL IN PEAK HILL, SYDENHAM, c. 1900, when it was a boarding school for girls, run by the Misses Levick. The house existed for a hundred years, from the 1850s to the 1950s. An earlier occupant, c. 1881, had been Lady Roberts, wife of the field marshall. Lord Bobs himself probably lived here for a time, but was more often overseas, empire-building.

ST MARGARET'S HIGHER GRADE SCHOOL occupied the extension behind the parish rooms at No. 50 Old Road, Lee (now a warehouse), c. 1889 to 1920. It was originally a girls' school, but had obviously compromised its standards by 1912, when this photograph was taken. The girl second from the right in the back row is thought to have been Freda Clark, later a well-known local dance teacher.

THE INTRODUCTION OF COMPETITIVE EXAMINATIONS gave rise to the new profession of army crammer, who coached candidates for Sandhurst and Woolwich. One of the best was Henry Wolffram, the man with the walrus moustache in this 1880s group of his students. They are posed before the east wing of The Manor House, Lee, a wing demolished in 1901. Wolffram was at Lee from 1877 to 1898. Three years later The Manor House became a public library; the Lewisham Local History Centre now occupies the first floor.

WHILE THE HABERDASHER ASKE'S GIRLS WERE IN WARTIME EXILE at Garnant in Carmarthenshire, their school at New Cross was not deserted. This dance on 3 September 1941 was one of a series given by the Mayor of Deptford for the borough's civil defence workers.

THE LEWISHAM GRAMMAR SCHOOL FOR GIRLS in Rushey Green is better known as Prendergast's school, after the Revd Joseph Prendergast (1791–1875), headmaster of Colfe's school, whose bequest of £6,000 formed the major part of its endowment. The school was opened on 17 July 1890. The identified members of the (all male) platform party were Theophilus William Williams, far left (see p. 73), the Hon. and Revd Canon Legge, Vicar of Lewisham, sixth from the left, and S.P. Low, the chairman of the governors, fifth from the right. The others included Michael Whitehall, who gave the stained-glass window, W.G. Lemon of the London County Council, A.L. Guy, the architect, and probably S.J. Jerrard, the builder. The *Kentish Mercury* recorded that 'Mr Hallier of High-street, Sydenham, took several photographs of the proceedings'. This is the only one known to have survived.

A CLASS BEING PUT THROUGH ITS MORNING DRILL at Monson Road higher grade school (near Millwall's ground, the Den), c. 1905. This was one of the many postcards printed in Germany during the Edwardian period. The discipline seems to have been imported from the same source.

THE VENUE WAS BROCKLEY ROAD SCHOOL, now Brockley junior and infant school, and the date probably c. 1910. But was it an art class, a rehearsal for the school play, or a group of trainee geisha girls?

THE LONDON COUNTY COUNCIL ran an open air school at Birley House, No. 108 London Road, c. 1910 to 1925. It was intended to strengthen delicate pupils, especially those from deprived homes, by exposing them to the bracing air of Forest Hill. Like Hans Castorp, they were expected to take regular outdoor naps (above), and were encouraged to pursue hobbies like gardening and the keeping of pets (right). Birley House was demolished in the 1920s, and the site incorporated in Horniman Gardens.

GOLDSMITHS' COLLEGE IN LEWISHAM WAY was built between 1843 and 1845 for the Royal Naval school. The architect was John Shaw, who most unusually for that period chose a Queen Anne style, the fine detail of which was spoilt by the destruction of the roof during the Second World War. In 1891 the Goldsmiths' Company opened the building as a 'technical and recreative institute' for the people of South London, but after fourteen years the expense proved too great even for them and they handed it over to the University of London. These photographs of 1906–7 show some of the original students under the new regime (the 'aborigines'), above, in the library, which was destroyed in the bombing, and, below, indulging in amateur dramatics, perhaps *The School for Scandal*.

THE GOLDSMITHS' COLLEGE SCHOOL OF ART was founded by the Goldsmiths' Company in 1891, and retained by the University of London after 1905. Among its students have been the novelists Jeffrey Farnol and Denton Welch, the poet and artist David Jones, the painter Graham Sutherland, and Tom Keating the faker. The photograph above shows a drawing class c. 1906. Below is the modelling studio before 1905. The positioning of the instructor's hands is in itself a Victorian work of art.

The World of Work

FENTON AND ASH'S FORGE, No. 61 Sangley Road, Catford, c. 1923.

LEWISHAM BRIDGE MILL IN MILL ROAD was almost certainly one of the eleven mills on the Ravensbourne mentioned in Domesday Book. It was used to grind corn for most of its long career, but had a brief period of glory in the middle of the eighteenth century when a leading London glass cutter, Thomas Betts, used it to manufacture his chandeliers, decanters, and other fine wares. This photograph was taken c. 1880 during the tenure of the flour millers J. and H. Robinson. They moved to Lewisham in the early 1850s, rebuilt the mill on the much larger scale seen here, and remained until 1920. After some years as a warehouse the mill was demolished in 1935. On the right is the sign of the Maid of the Mill (see p. 55). Mill Road and its vicinity was Lewisham's red-light district, known almost officially as Botany Bay.

LOAMPIT HILL takes its name from the quarrying and brickmaking industries carried on there during the eighteenth and nineteenth centuries. One of the brickworks was George Faulkner's, established c. 1825. His kiln was on a site now enclosed by Shell, Fossil and Brookbank Roads. Henry Wood's photograph shows it in the late 1850s, when it was still known as Faulkner's, although the business had been taken over by Benjamin Parkes c. 1850.

SOME OF THE YOUNG BRICKMAKERS employed at Heath's Crofton Park Brick Works during the 1890s. Job Heath was the tenant of College Farm, next to The Brockley Jack, c. 1889 to 1891, when he established his works in Holdenby Road. He was only there for about five years, but in that time he produced the bricks with which large areas of Crofton Park and Ladywell were built.

HOLLETT'S FORGE AND BRASHER'S BUILDERS YARD occupied these premises at No. 40A Turner Road, Lee, later known as No. 13 Dacre Park, for more than fifty years. Stephen Hollett, the central figure in the group below, ran the blacksmith's business c. 1887 to 1918, and his widow continued it into the 1930s. David Brasher began the building firm c. 1893, and it survived until the Second World War.

THE WORKING RIVER IN 1898. This collier was moored off William Dowell and Co.'s coal depot at Creek Bridge Wharf, Norway Street, on the Greenwich bank of Deptford Creek. Dowell's, a firm with offices all over Lewisham and Deptford, used a short railway to move the coal from the river to the waiting carts.

A PICTURE OF A CHANGING WORLD. These garages behind the Golden Lion in Sydenham Road were old stables, and the chauffeur was probably an old coachman. Yet at the back of the building on the right John Edney, one of a long-established family of Sydenham blacksmiths, still had a forge.

THERE WERE WAREHOUSES FOR NAVAL STORES at Deptford by 1513, and it continued to be an important depot for the navy's private victualling contractors until the yard was enlarged and established on an official footing in 1742. It received the name of the Royal Victoria Yard in 1858, after a visit by the queen. In the late nineteenth century it employed more than four hundred hands, some of them seen above leaving by the main gate in Grove Street at knocking-off time. The yard closed in 1961, and the Pepys housing estate has been built on the site. These gates have been retained, as have a number of the warehouses and officers' residences. (See also p. 153.) The crafts at the Royal Victoria Yard maintained their traditions to the last. The photograph (left) of the passing-out ceremony of an apprentice cooper, an arduous process involving tarring and feathering, was taken only about ten years before the yard was closed.

A PRIZE BULL which had just arrived at the foreign cattle market, Deptford, for one of the Christmas sales, c. 1900. Between 1871 and 1913 the market occupied the former royal dockyard, and these cattle pens were in an old shipbuilding shed. One of them still survives on the site, now the premises of a newsprint importer.

THE ORIGINAL PICTURE is captioned 'a boilermaker in Hughes Fields, Deptford', but it is more likely that he was employed around the corner at John Penn's great marine boiler works in Butchers Row and Watergate Street. The date was perhaps in the 1890s.

LAUREL COTTAGE IN RUSHEY GREEN was one of Lewisham's most short-lived houses. It was built in the early 1870s, and demolished in 1889, when the site was required for Prendergast's school (see p. 96). The only known tenant was the one seen here, C.T. Williams, the job master, who fulfilled for the age of the horse many of the functions of the modern car hire and removals firms.

THE RIVERDALE MILL survives as a museum piece in Molesworth Street, with the electrically powered wheel now turning the water! The photograph shows it in 1898, when it was a flour mill.

THE GAS WORKS AT BELL GREEN, Sydenham began as the home of the Crystal Palace Gas Company in 1858. At least two labourers at the works have gained some celebrity. One was Henry Cooper, the other William Bottle (right), who worked in the retort house from 1891 to 1901, when he was discovered by a music hall talent scout. Using the stage name of 'Datas', Bottle had great success with an act like that of Mr Memory in Hitchcock's *39 Steps*. During the First World War the gasworks lost most of its regular staff, and women (seen below, with two token males) were recruited to fill the gaps.

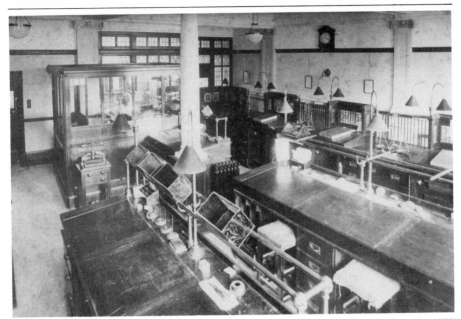

THE INTERIOR OF THE LONDON, COUNTY, AND WESTMINSTER BANK (now the Nat West) at Nos 157 and 159 Rushey Geen, photographed c. 1917. It occupies the site of the old Catford police station (see p. 112).

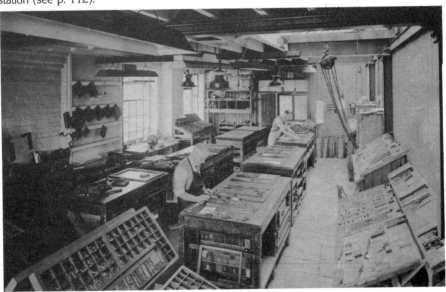

THIS PHOTOGRAPH WAS TAKEN IN JUNE 1953, but modern developments make it seem as quaint as an alchemist's laboratory. It was the composing room of the Lewisham Newspaper Company, which produced the *Lewisham Borough News*. It ceased publication in 1975, and the offices in Algernon Road are now a work experience centre.

Servants of the Public

THE KITCHENS OF LEWISHAM HOSPITAL in 1922.

NOT THE SET OF A MACK SENNETT COMEDY, but the Catford police station in Rushey Green (see also p. 59) in 1850, or a few years later. The large numbers are accounted for by the fact that this was a punishment station. Delinquent bobbies were sent here from all over London, to recover their characters in the peace and innocence of the countryside.

SOCIAL CHANGE MIGHT PERHAPS BE PLOTTED through the architecture of police stations. This charming cottage in Dartmouth Road (seen here c. 1902) served Sydenham from 1848 until 1966, when it was replaced on a greatly expanded site by the present grim barracks.

HENRY COCKLE, BEADLE OF ST PAUL'S, Deptford in the 1860s and '70s, was an exuberant character. In 1868 he was reported dead, but proved the rumour was exaggerated by appearing in the 'High Street next day in all the glory of scarlett, buff, and gold'. The next year, when his wife died, he had the opposite problem, because all the world insisted she was only in a trance, and the funeral had to be delayed for several weeks. He is best remembered for his exhortation to the rector, when insulted by roughs: 'You are not going to allow that, Governor, are you? Let the buggers have it!'. The scarlet breeches and waistcoat he is wearing in this portrait are preserved at the Lewisham Local History Centre.

SOME OF THE TOWN CLERK'S STAFF at work, c. 1905, in the Metropolitan Borough of Deptford's original offices at No. 50 Tanners Hill. The mayor described them as 'the nearest approach to a black hole into which a body of administrators were ever thrust'. They were used from 1900 to 1905, when the town hall was completed. The building, which had previously been the headquarters of the St Paul's vestry, still survives.

THE GUESTS, WHO INCLUDED SIDNEY WEBB, assembling for the opening ceremony of Deptford Town Hall on 19 July 1905. This fine building was once described as 'obscene', not because of the statuary, which is impeccably dressed in historic naval costumes, but because its luxury contrasted so strongly with the poverty of the borough.

SEVERE FLOODS STRUCK PARTS OF DEPTFORD on 7 January 1928. Here council officers are seen distributing blankets to victims in Grove Street.

THIS WAS LEWISHAM'S THIRD FIRE STATION, built on the site of Lewisham House (see p. 43), and opened in 1898. The photograph was taken about ten years later. It was replaced by a fourth station on the other side of the High Street in 1967, but the old building still survives.

LEWISHAM'S FIRST PUBLIC LIBRARY, at Perry Hill, lasted only from 1891 until 1901, when it was superseded by the purpose-built Central and Forest Hill libraries. The building was an old chapel and lecture hall. It already had a stock of 4,000 volumes, which the poorly-funded library service gladly took over. This early 1890s photograph shows all the staff except C.W.F. Goss, the librarian, who was perhaps behind the camera. The man in the foreground was his deputy, W. Fortune. The old library survived until c. 1965 as a public hall. The builder's yard next door, then Alfred Sykes's, is now that of Walker, Clinging.

A PRIZE-WINNING LEWISHAM STREET-CLEANING TEAM in 1904. The neatness of their turnout may have been connected with a council plan at that time to economize by reducing the number of dustmen.

MAYOW ROAD, SYDENHAM being resurfaced in the 1920s by the Vialit Reconditioning Process, which promised 'new roads from old'. The house in the background was St Monica's. Its gate is on the right. The small gate on the left was the back entrance to St Magnus in Dacres Road.

LEWISHAM WORKHOUSE AND INFIRMARY in 1898, a scene scarcely changed nearly a hundred years later. The workhouse block of 1817 (on the extreme left of the photograph) and the various extensions built between 1882 and 1894, now form the major part of Lewisham Hospital. There are more modern additions to the north and west.

NURSES OF THE SYDENHAM CHILDRENS' HOSPITAL (see also p. 144), c. 1920. It was founded in 1872 in Sydenham Park by Mr and Mrs Edmund Chapman and Mrs Chapman's sister, Miss E.C. Elwes, and moved to Champion Hall, Sydenham Road, in 1885. This was one of the charities supported by the Hospitals Welfare Society (see p. 33). It was demolished in 1991.

SECTION TWELVE

Places to Go

F.J. HORNIMAN'S OLD HOME, Surrey Mount, as the refreshment room of Horniman's Gardens, Forest Hill.

THE BANK HOLIDAY FUNFAIRS on Blackheath were huge events, with up to a thousand stalls and sideshows straggling for a mile along Shooters Hill Road, and sometimes as many as fifty thousand visitors from all over South London. This postcard of the swingboats was issued c. 1905. By then the London County Council had acted to reduce the event to some extent, but it was still immensely popular.

GWENNIE AND DORIS TUCKER of Tucker's cash drug store (see p. 135) paying their pennies to the roundabout attendant at Blackheath funfair in 1915. In the background is Greenwich Park.

THE NEW CROSS EMPIRE VARIETY THEATRE stood opposite the Addey and Stanhope school in New Cross Road. It opened in 1899, and was for many years one of the leading suburban music halls. The George Formby topping the bill at the time of this 1912 postcard was the father of the ukulele strummer. The Empire closed in 1954, a victim of television, and was demolished in 1958.

THE FLAMBOYANT BROADWAY THEATRE, which was designed by W.G.R. Sprague, stood at the corner of New Cross Road and Tanners Hill from 1897 until 1963. It was intended primarily for straight drama, but, almost from the first, showed films as well. These proved the greater attraction, and the Broadway became a full-time cinema in 1916.

SOME OF THE FIFTEEN-THOUSAND-STRONG CROWD who watched a minute-by-minute re-enactment of the 1909 boat race by cardboard boats on the front of Sainsbury's Lewisham store. As the information was updated 'by telephonic communication', one young Oxford fan was so excited that he fell over the railings into the Quaggy River. But perhaps the novelty was already fading: the 1908 event had attracted nearly thirty thousand spectators.

THE GILD HALL IN LEWISHAM HIGH STREET, at the corner of Courthill Road, was built in 1911 as a temperance billiard room. A contemporary note on the back of this card of c.1912 describes it as 'a lovely café with music and fountain in center & behind about 28 billiard tables. Such a big place.' It is now a bingo club.

FREDERICK JOHN HORNIMAN, MP (1835–1906), the tea merchant, lived at Surrey Mount, Forest Hill (see p. 119). He collected large numbers of artefacts and curios on his extensive travels, and in 1890 opened Surrey House, No. 100 London Road, to show them to the public. The collection continued to grow, so between 1897 and 1901 he built the existing Horniman's Museum on the site of Surrey House. It was designed by Harrison Townsend, and is regarded as one of the finest buildings of its date in the country. The photograph on the left shows the progress of the work in July 1899. Below, Horniman is seen with the original staff in May 1903. The porters in the back row were (left to right): Messrs Hancock, Finnigan, Oborne, Nicholls, Sutton, and Wilkes. In the front row were Frank Slade, the natural history assistant, Richard Quick, the resident curator, Horniman, and A.W. Pepper, the librarian.

124

MARIE LLOYD and most of the other great stars of music hall trod the boards of the Lewisham Hippodrome in Rushey Green, seen here shortly after its opening in 1911. It also featured opera and straight drama, and had two periods as a cinema, from 1931 to 1933, and after 1952, when it was renamed The Eros. It closed in 1959, and was demolished the next year. The site, at the corner of Brownhill Road, is now occupied by a hideous tower called Eros House.

THE EXOTIC KING'S HALL CINEMA at the top of Lewisham High Street, not long after it opened in December 1912. After bomb damage in 1940 and 1943 it was reconstructed in a plainer style, and became first The Rex and then Studios 6 and 7. It was demolished a few years ago.

THE CENTRAL HALL SKATING RINK and the Catford Picture Palace in Sangley Road late in 1911, when Italy and Turkey were at war. The cinema opened in 1909, the first purpose-built one in Lewisham or Deptford, and was so popular that in 1911 an open-air annexe was needed. The Palace closed in 1914, after its owner had built the larger Central Hall cinema (now the Cannon) next door. It survives as a furniture showroom, as does the skating rink.

THE LEWISHAM ELECTRIC PALACE in August or September 1911. The cinema opened in 1909, and lasted until 1922, when it was rebuilt as The Prince of Wales. That was demolished in 1960, and the Homestyle and Beatties shops are now on the High Street site.

THE CAFETERIA OF THE NEW CROSS KINEMA in 1927 – two years after the opening – when it was showing Alfred Hitchcock's first big hit. This was the borough's biggest silent cinema, with seating for thirteen hundred, a dance hall, and an orchestra of twenty. It closed in 1960, and the building, at the corner of New Cross Road and Clifton Rise, is now converted into shops.

WHEN THE GAUMONT PALACE, at the corner of Loampit Vale and Lewisham High Street, opened in 1932, it was one of the finest cinemas in London. This postcard shows it in its pristine glory in June 1933, and makes a sad contrast with its recent appearance. The Gaumont became The Odeon in 1962, closed in 1981 and was demolished in 1991.

MOUNTSFIELD WAS BUILT IN 1845, as a wedding present to the entomologist Henry Tibbats Stainton (1822–92) from his father. When Mrs Stainton died the local market for such estates had vanished, and in 1903 it was made into a public park. The house, found unsuitable for an industrial school or library, was demolished in 1905, but these outbuildings were retained. The stables (centre), largely destroyed by fire in 1969, became the park keeper's headquarters. The museum (left) which Stainton built for his specimens c. 1860, became the refreshment room. It was demolished in 1981.

THIS, WHICH LOOKS LIKE EVERY ENTERTAINER'S IDEAL AUDIENCE, was assembled at the Forster Memorial Park in Whitefoot Lane during August 1948, to enjoy Clown Moore's Punch and Judy show.

SECTION THIRTEEN

Shopping

PEPPERCORN'S DEPARTMENT STORE in Deptford Broadway (see p. 131), c. 1900.

WHEN THIS PHOTOGRAPH WAS TAKEN, C. 1903, Lewisham's street market occupied only the southern half of its present site. The view is northwards towards Avenue Road (later Romer Avenue, and now the central walkway of the Lewisham Centre), where the market then ended. Kerswell's piano shop at the corner of Avenue Road was better known under its later name of Murdoch's.

JAMES COLLINGWOOD ESTABLISHED HIS DRAPERY SHOP on the site now occupied by Marks and Spencer in the early 1870s. It was the largest in Lewisham until overtaken by Chiesman's. This photograph of C. 1900 shows the view southwards towards the Avenue Road corner, with the street market beyond. In the distance is the spire of the Lewisham Congregational church.

THIS CHEMIST'S SHOP at the corner of Lewisham High Street and Lewis Grove was founded by Thomas Wyborne in 1835. Edward Clift acquired the business in 1848, and took E.L. Crow into partnership in 1868. It survived until 1897, shortly after which the premises were demolished and the London, City and Midland Bank (now the Midland) was built on the site.

PEPPERCORN'S CARPET SHOWROOM in the 1890s. Joseph Peppercorn opened a small grocery shop on the north side of Deptford Broadway in 1822, and gradually expanded in both directions until the business grew to the size shown in the photograph on p. 129. By the 1890s there was also a shop in Deptford High Street (see p. 29), and a branch at Greenwich, and Peppercorn's had become a comprehensive department store. It closed in 1916.

THESE PROPERTIES IN NEW CROSS ROAD (seen here in 1872) were built c. 1854. Those on the right were known as Hamilton Terrace West until they were converted into shops in 1871. All were destroyed during the Second World War, and new shops have been built on the site, just west of Pagnell Street. William Kipps, the musical instruments dealer, was organist of St Paul's, Greenwich, and publisher of *The Minim*, a musical magazine. Did his fame stretch as far as Bromley and H.G. Wells?

MRS J. MAUDE AND JESSIE LIDDELL ran this shop at No. 21 Lee High Road (now Centrepoint) from 1918 to 1949. The houses behind, Mount Eliot Villa and Mount Eliot House, were built c. 1850, as part of the original Marischal Road development. The shopfronts were added in the 1880s.

THE PART OF KIRKDALE between Sydenham station and Westwood Hill, *c.* 1908. The old station entrance on the left was demolished some years ago. The shops were built in the 1870s. The white-painted pair formed Cobb's furnishing department, an annexe to the main store opposite. The shop to their left (now the excellent Kirkdale Bookshop) was later also absorbed by Cobb's. The delivery cart belonged to Chalk and Cox, the butchers (right).

ONE OF WALTER COBB'S DELIVERY CARTS, *c.* 1905. Cobb's, which was Sydenham's only department store, was founded in 1860. That is the date on the shop still dominating Cobb's Corner in Kirkdale, though in fact it was rebuilt in 1902, and originally bore that date. Cobb's closed in 1981.

A FAR CRY from the modern conception of a Sainsbury's store, but this little shop at No. 30A Catford Hill served the firm well from c. 1900 until the late 1950s. It is now occupied by Catford Bridge Motors. The year of the photograph is harder to estimate than the month, but it was probably taken c. 1905.

JOHN SAMUEL SMITH at the door of No. 20 Perry Hill during the 1890s. He had established himself as a grocer in Perry Hill in the 1840s, and moved to this new shop c. 1880. It was demolished in the 1960s. The post office had Perry Hill Library (see p. 116) on one side and Burgoyne's forge on the other. It is to be hoped that the advertisements for Burgoyne's wines were only a coincidence.

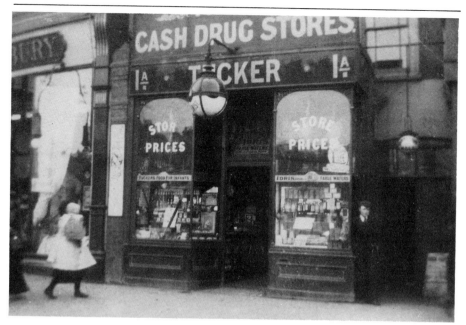

WILLIAM TUCKER FOUNDED HIS CASH DRUG STORES (above) at No. 1A Obelisk Buildings, later No. 1A Loampit Vale, in 1891. The shop was next to Sainsbury's, at the corner of Lewisham High Street (see p. 123). In 1912 the business moved to No. 9A Loampit Vale, at the corner of Molesworth Street, and it is the interior of this second shop which is shown in the photograph below. (See also p. 120.)

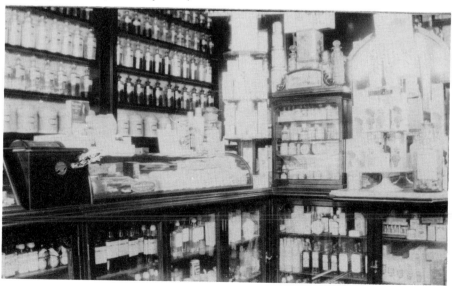

THE SOUTHERN END OF LEWISHAM ROAD seen from the corner of Granville Park during a Lewisham Traders' Exhibition, c. 1918. Mrs Cecelia Snow ran her sweet shop at No. 190 (now No. 310) Lewisham Road c. 1903 to 1921.

THE BOTTOM OF LEWISHAM HIGH STREET, c. 1908. On the right is George Lane, and part of the sign of the George Inn. These shops were built c. 1900 on the site of a fine old house called The Maples. The Catford Bon Marché was the fancy name for William Anthony Mathew's drapery business.

IN THE FIRST HALF OF THE TWENTIETH CENTURY the grocery chain of Cave, Austin, was one of the largest in the south-east. In the 1920s they built this warehouse at No. 34 Eastdown Park to supply their branches in Kentish London.

AN EARLY CHIESMANS' DELIVERY VAN. The Chiesman brothers created Lewisham's greatest department store. They began modestly in 1884 with a single fancy draper's shop, called the Paris House, next to Maller's on the High Pavement (see p. 32), but within eight years had absorbed most of their neighbours. They eventually rebuilt the main block, and extended across Granville Grove all the way to St Stephen's. The store became the Army and Navy in 1983.

HERBERT FUDGE at the door of his newsagent's shop at No. 313 Lee High Road (now a private house), probably in June 1927. His lugubrious expression seems to foretell little good for *The Happy Mag*. Fudge began his career in 1907 as a barber at No. 327 Lee High Road, drifted into his more natural line, and moved to this shop in 1913. His family continued the business until the late 1950s.

Distinguished Visitors

KING GEORGE VI AND QUEEN ELIZABETH at Deptford on 14 June 1940.

THE FUTURE EDWARD VII AND QUEEN ALEXANDRA were at Deptford on 1 July 1898 to lay the foundation stone of the Albany Institute in Creek Road, which was named after their sister-in-law, the Duchess of Albany. She was the very active president of the Deptford Fund, the charity of which this was the new headquarters. The prince caused some controversy by condemning the indifference of Brockley and Hatcham, the wealthy fringes, to the poverty of inner Deptford.

Previous page:
THE PRINCE AND PRINCESS OF WALES, afterwards Edward VII and Queen Alexandra, visited Lewisham on 12 July 1897 to open the Park Hospital at Hither Green. 'With a view to gratifying as large a number of residents in the district as possible' the royal party travelled via New Cross Road, Lewisham High Road (now Lewisham Way), Loampit Hill, Lewisham High Street, Lewisham Park, Thornford Road, and Hither Green Lane; and returned along Rushey Green, Stanstead Road, and London Road, accompanied all the way by a splendid mounted escort of the West Kent Yeomanry. All the schools in Deptford and Lewisham declared a half-holiday, and large crowds gathered along the route, but the police reported no trouble, except for the reckless behaviour of certain cyclists. The clock tower was not built until later in the year, so that in this picture of the modern market area there is an uninterrupted view of the High Pavement (see p. 32). Note that the two leading High Pavement shops, Chiesmans' and Stroud's, both had advertisements on the well-placed horse tram.

WHEN THE PRINCE AND PRINCESS OF WALES, on 12 July 1900, opened St Olave's workhouse, or 'home of rest for the aged and infirm poor' as the prince preferred to call it, huge crowds gathered to welcome them. 'The weather', the local paper wryly commented, 'was really royal – for once in a way on an occasion of the sort – brilliant sunshine playing upon the bunting.' This was the animated scene in Ladywell Road, just outside the workhouse entrance. The Ladywell Tavern is on the extreme right of the picture. (See also p. 52.)

MOST OF SYDENHAM TURNED OUT on 12 March 1926 when Queen Mary opened the new nurses' home at the South Eastern Hospital for Children (see p. 118). She is seen here being greeted by Sir Philip Dawson, MP for West Lewisham.

THE DUKE OF YORK, afterwards King George VI, outside the Lewisham town hall extension at Catford, shortly before declaring it open on 22 June 1932. Why were his sinister detectives looking so anxious? See the photograph opposite.

THE CRUSH OUTSIDE THE TOWN HALL on 22 June 1932, when half of Lewisham came to see the Duke of York, and the St John's Ambulance Brigade were kept busy dealing with those who fainted. The hatless eccentrics in the crowd look inappropriately sheepish. Behind the tram is St Laurence's church, which was demolished in 1968 to make way for a further extension to the town hall, now rapidly nearing completion. Will the present Duke of York be asked to open it?

KING GEORGE VI AND QUEEN ELIZABETH visiting an air raid shelter in Vesta Road, Brockley, on 14 June 1940. 'His Majesty was particular pleased with this shelter, which is built like a tramcar, with a gangway between the seats. One almost expects a conductor to come along and request "Fares please".'

DURING THEIR VICTORY TOUR on 10 May 1945 King George VI, Queen Elizabeth, and the two princesses stopped in Lewisham High Street at the spot were the flying bomb had fallen ten months earlier (see p. 156). The bomb site behind the royal car was between the High Street and Lewis Grove, with the ruins of the Albion pub on the right.

HERBERT MORRISON, LATER LORD MORRISON OF LAMBETH, was a Lewisham MP from 1945 to 1959. He is seen above in 1950 (when he was leader of the House of Commons) dancing with the Mayoress of Lewisham, Mrs Moys, at the mayor's Jubilee Dance. The mayor is dancing with Mrs Morrison. Below, at a Lewisham Labour Party guest night on 24 September 1960 (also held at Lewisham Concert Hall), Lord Morrison is chatting with Hugh Gaitskell, the man who beat him in the party leadership election in 1955. The book is Morrison's autobiography, hot off the press.

DURING THE GENERAL ELECTION CAMPAIGN of October 1964 the leaders of both the main parties visited Lewisham High Street. Sir Alec Douglas-Home (above), then prime minister, is seen speaking outside St Stephen's church on 3 July in support of the athlete Christopher Chattaway, MP for Lewisham North from 1959 to 1966. Harold Wilson held his meeting (below) in the playground of St Mary's schools on 19 September.

Two World Wars

GROVE PARK HOSPITAL as an Army Service Corps barracks during the First World War.

MEMBERS OF LEWISHAM BATTALION OF THE NATIONAL RESERVE at the Catford-Southend Football Club stadium in Mountsfield Park on 6 June 1914, before a fund-raising procession to Forest Hill. They were dressed in historic British army uniforms. Living antiquities present included Crimea and Indian Mutiny veterans, and Sergeant Farrow, a survivor of Rorke's Drift. The Catford-Southend ground was the home of Charlton Athletic during the 1922/3 season, when the Robins made one of their periodic attempts to fly from The Valley.

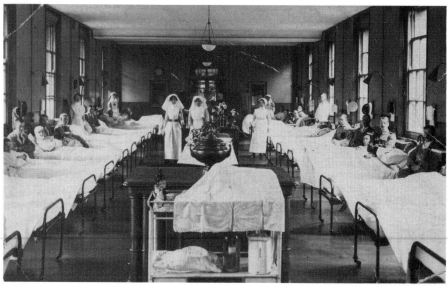

LIFE MUST HAVE BEEN HARD FOR LEWISHAM'S CIVILIANS who fell ill during the First World War, when most of the local hospitals were taken over by the military. These are the nurses and patients of Lewisham Hospital's Albert Ward.

DURING THE FIRST WORLD WAR Deptford Council was very energetic in recruiting soldiers. Here, probably in 1915, are two of the local outfits on parade. Above, the 179th Deptford Gun Brigade at the old John Penn works in Blackheath Road. Below, probably the 174th Deptford Gun Brigade at the Evelyn Street tramway depot. The houses behind, since demolished, were in Crooke Road.

POTATO SHORTAGES were a serious civilian hardship of the First World War. This potato queue is outside No. 172 Manor Lane, Lee, the shop of Charles Fowler, greengrocer, coal merchant, and removal man. On the left is No. 107 Fernbrook Road, and part of the railway bridge.

THE DEPTFORD RED CROSS PAGEANT on 20 October 1917 featured floats representing, somewhat in the taste of the Albert Memorial, the British Empire and its allies. This is the French float.

THE ROYAL VICTORIA YARD AT DEPTFORD decorated to celebrate the end of the First World War in November 1918, though for the men the rejoicing may have been half-hearted, as peace was apt to be the forerunner of redundancies. The yard (for which see also p. 106) not only stored, but produced or processed much of the navy's rations. These 1780s riverside buildings (now converted into flats on the Pepys Estate) were, left to right, the peas and beans store, the chief office, the superintendent's house, and the rum store. The largest rum vat held some 32,000 gallons.

DURING THE MUNICH AUTUMN of 1938 strange things were happening in open spaces all over London. In Deptford Park they were busy digging these trench shelters, while Chamberlain was building castles in the air.

Hitler yells on the wireless,
The night is damp and still
And I hear dull blows on wood
outside my window;
They are cutting down the trees
on Primrose Hill.

ROLLING FOR VICTORY? Two Deptford air raid wardens, Mrs R. Lowe and Mr H. Berquez, gardening at No. 82 Wickham Road, then wardens' post No. 19, on 20 June 1941.

DEPTFORD TOWN HALL (see p. 114) in 1940, boarded-up and heavily protected by sandbags. This was the control centre for the borough's civil defence and anti-air-raid work.

TWENTY-TWO PEOPLE WERE KILLED when Reginald Square, a late 1850s development behind the north side of Deptford Broadway, was destroyed by a flying bomb on 16 June 1944, the first night of the VI bombardment. This photograph was taken shortly afterwards. The two landmarks in the background were the spire of St Paul's, Deptford, and the chimney of a soap factory in Frankham Street.

THE SCENE IN LEWISHAM HIGH STREET after a flying bomb had fallen on 28 July 1944, killing fifty-one and injuring hundreds. Many of the casualties were in the shelter under the street market, which took the full impact of the bomb. This is the same view, from a higher angle, as in the photograph on pp. 140 and 141, and the lower postcard on p. 32. A number of the Victorian shops on the left of those pictures had been rebuilt in the 1920s and '30s, so now the likes of Marks and Spencer had to start again. The area on the right, between the High Street and Lewis Grove (see pp. 27 and 146), was also devastated, and it was not until the 1950s that Lewisham's main shopping centre was fully restored. The Albion pub was eventually rebuilt, but has now been converted into a branch of the Abbey National.

BY THE BEGINNING OF 1944 air raids had decreased so much that on 6 January Deptford Council decided to test its street lighting. It was an entirely new experience for the younger of these children from Malpas Road, Brockley.

WHAT THE LOCAL HISTORIAN WOULD CALL THE IDEAL PHOTOGRAPH, leaving him to say only that Geraint Road is on the Downham Estate, and that Victory in Europe day was 8 May 1945.

THE WAR IS WON, and all over Britain bulldozers and cranes are busy knocking down air raid shelters. This version of the familiar scene is being enacted in Taunton Road, Lee.

IN THE AFTERMATH OF WAR, a National Service Medical Board meets at Blackheath Concert Hall, c. 1954, to decide the fates of some of the unfortunate young men called up for military duty. The board member standing far left is identified as Dr Pilsworth, an excellent name. The concert hall, built in 1895, was requisitioned for government use in 1940, and has only lately been returned to its proper function.

ACKNOWLEDGEMENTS

For permission to reproduce copyright photographs, and for other valuable assistance and advice, I have to thank the London Borough of Lewisham; its Local History Centre at The Manor House, Old Road, Lee, London, SE13, and the archivist, Mr Carl Harrison; Mr K. George; and Mr A.M. Riley, who has tried to guide my innocent steps through the complexities of railway history. If I have still made mistakes, the fault is mine, not his.

In my notes on early cinemas I have relied with confidence on Ken George's authoritative work, *Two Sixpennies, Please* (1987). For Blackheath information I have turned, as everybody must, to Neil Rhind's definitive volumes, *Blackheath Village and Environs* (vols 1 and 2, 1976 and 1983), and *The Heath* (1987). In dealing with the Second World War bombing of Lewisham I have raided *Red Alert* by Lewis Blake (1982). I can unreservedly recommend all of these publications.

Finally, my thanks to Mr Kenneth Clark, the editor of the companion volume, *Greenwich and Woolwich in Old Photographs.* It was he who first suggested that I should undertake this task, and he has thus treated me to a summer full of interest and amusement.

For corrections in this reprint I am grateful to Mr Alfred Wood and Mr W.J. Seaman.